What is a
Self-Portrait?

Ruth Thomson

SEA-TO-SEA
Mankato Collingwood London

This edition first published in 2006 by
Sea-to-Sea Publications
1980 Lookout Drive
North Mankato
Minnesota 56003

Library of Congress Cataloging-in-Publication Data:

Thomson, Ruth, 1949-
    What is a self-portrait? / by Ruth Thomson.
        p. cm. — (Art's alive!)
    Includes index.
    ISBN 1-932889-89-2
    1. Self-portraits—Juvenile literature. I. Title. II. Art's alive! (North Mankato, Minn.)

N7618.T5 2005
704.9"42—dc22

2004062733

9 8 7 6 5 4 3 2

Published by arrangement with the Watts Publishing Group Ltd, London

Editor: Caryn Jenner
Design: Sphere Design
Art director: Jonathan Hair
Photography: Ray Moller
Picture research: Diana Morris

The publisher wishes to thank Fiona Cole for her assistance with the artwork and activities in this book.
Thanks also to the children who contributed artwork for the activities: Kwame Bumbury-Lindsay, Madeleine Hennessy, and Imani Jawarah.

Acknowledgments: Alte Pinakothek, Munich/Bridgeman Art Library: 24. El Prado, Madrid/Joseph Martin/The Art Archive: 23. El Prado, Madrid/Bridgeman Art Library: 17. Galleria degli Uffizi, Florence/Bridgeman Art Library: 9. Kenwood House, London/Bridgeman Art Library: 25. Chris Fairclough Colour Library: 21tl, 21tr. Kunstindustrimuseet, Copenhagen. Pernille Klemp: 19. Peter Millard: 20bl. Musée Cantini, Marseille. Photographie Jean Bernard © ADAGP, Paris & DACS, London 2004: 15. Musée d'Orsay, Paris/Gianni Dagli Orti/Corbis: front cover main, 11. Museo Correr, Venice/Bridgeman Art Library: 18. Museum of Modern Art, New York/Scala Archives.© ADAGP, Paris & DACS, London 2004: 27.

Artwork: Deborah Allwright: 12tl. Fiona Cole: cover tl, 7, 28br. Jacqueline East: 13. Martin Impey: title page and 12r. Barbara Vagnozzi: 22l. Lisa Williams: 12bl, 28bl.

Every attempt has been made to clear copyright. Should there be any inadvertent omission please apply to the publisher for rectification.

Contents

What is a self-portrait?

A self-portrait is a picture that an artist makes of herself or himself.

◄ Looking at myself
Artists often use a mirror to study themselves. They can copy the way they look, or change it.

Study yourself
What do you notice first when you look at yourself in a mirror? Do you notice your eyes, your hair, or the shape of your face?

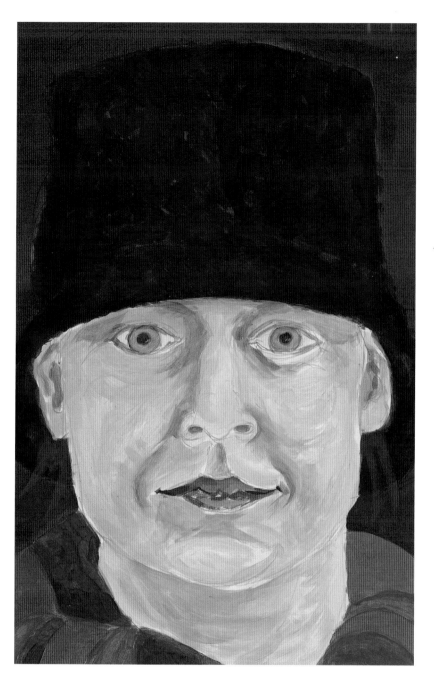

◀ *Self-portrait,*
Fiona Cole, 2004

Sometimes, artists just show their head and shoulders. This is the finished self-portrait that is being painted by the artist on the opposite page.

How is the artist's self-portrait different from her **reflection** in the mirror?

Faces

Everybody's face is different. Artists notice the shape and size of **features**, such as the eyes, nose, and mouth.

▲ **Front view**
You see the shape of a face from the front. Notice the shape and size of the eyes and mouth.

▲ **Side view**
From the side, you see the shape of the head, nose, chin, and forehead. A side view is called a **profile**.

My face
Draw a self-portrait that shows the shape of your face and the color of your hair and eyes.

▲ *Self-portrait*, Elizabeth Vigée-Lebrun, 1790

What do you notice about this artist's face?
Are her eyes big or small?
Is her chin wide or narrow?
Is her hair straight or curly?

Feelings

Artists can use different colors and marks to show how they are feeling.

How do they feel?
Notice how people's features change with their feelings.

△ This happy girl smiles, stretching her mouth wide.

△ This boy's eyes are open wide in surprise. See his raised eyebrows.

△ This girl's eyes and mouth turn down in sadness.

Happy and sad
Draw a happy and a sad self-portrait. Show your feelings with different marks—thick, thin, wiggly, dotty, or swirly.

How does this swirly background
show how the artist is feeling?

▲ *Self-portrait*, Vincent van Gogh, 1889

Van Gogh often used yellow to show
happiness. Why do you think he used
shades of blue for this self-portrait?

This is me

Sometimes artists add extras
to their self-portraits to tell you
more about themselves.

Clues about the artist
What can you guess about these
artists from the things they have
included in their self-portraits?

My favorite things
Draw your self-portrait.
Include some things that
show people what you like.

▲ *Self-portrait*, Jacqueline East, 2003

It is easy to see what this artist likes!

Pretending

Artists can show themselves
in an **imaginary** way.

◀ **Dressing up**
What do you think
this artist would
like to be?

Animal pictures
Imagine that part of
you has changed into
an animal. Draw a
picture of how you
might look.

What is strange about the creature that the artist is holding?

▲ *Autoportrait Impérial*,
Victor Brauner, 1947

In this self-portrait, the artist imagines he is like an eagle, with a big, beady eye, strong hands, and a feathery headdress. Look at his tiny, birdlike legs and feet.

Showing off

Artists sometimes use a self-portrait to celebrate an event or to show off a talent.

My birthday
The picture has a clue which tells you how old this boy is.

I'm a star
What do you think this boy likes doing?

About me
Draw a self-portrait of you doing something you enjoy. Think what you will wear and what you will hold.

▲ *Self-portrait*, Albrecht Dürer, 1498

Here, Dürer shows off his good looks
and expensive clothes, as well as his skill
in painting everything in very fine **detail**.

Sculpted self-portraits

Some artists make **sculptures** of themselves.
You can see a sculpture from all sides.
A sculpted head is called a **bust**.

◀ *Self-portrait,*
Antonio Canova, 1812
This artist carved his
bust from a hard stone
called marble.

A clay self-portrait
Use self-hardening
clay to **model** your
face. Paint it once it
is hard and dry.

▲ *Jug in the form of a head,*
Paul Gauguin, 1889
Gauguin modeled his head in clay.
He left the inside hollow and added
a handle to turn his self-portrait into a jug.

Photos

Today, some artists take photographs of themselves instead of painting a self-portrait.

Say cheese!
Hold a camera at arm's length and take a snap of yourself. Try to hold the camera steady.

Face the camera
Ask a friend to take a photo portrait of you. Think about how to **pose** and what **expression** to make.

◣ Dressing up

You could dress up for
a photo and include
pets, food, or toys.

◣ Acting up

You could pretend to
be scared, sad, brave,
or excited!

Friends ▶
Choose a
good pose for
a photo of
you and your
best friend.

Family portraits

Artists may include their families in their self-portraits.

▲ *Self-portrait,*
Barbara Vagnozzi, 2003
What clues has this artist included to show that she is both a mother and an artist?

Me and my family
Draw a picture of you with your family. Think how you will group everyone in the picture, and what they will wear.

What pets does this family have?

▲ *The artist and his family in a garden,*
Jacob Jordaens, about 1621

You can't tell that the man who painted this
picture was an artist. Instead, he shows
himself as a rich, well-dressed gentleman
with his wife and child, and even a maid.

Different ages

Some artists paint self-portraits throughout their lives, from young to old.

◀ *Self-portrait as a young man*, Rembrandt van Rijn, 1629

Rembrandt painted 80 self-portraits at different times in his life. This one shows him as a young man. He looks as if he is in a hurry.

What differences can you see between the two paintings?

▲ *Self-portrait,*
Rembrandt van Rijn, 1661-62

Rembrandt painted this portrait when he was old. By then, he was very famous.

Past and present

Sometimes, artists show what they are like now and what they were like in the past—both in the same painting.

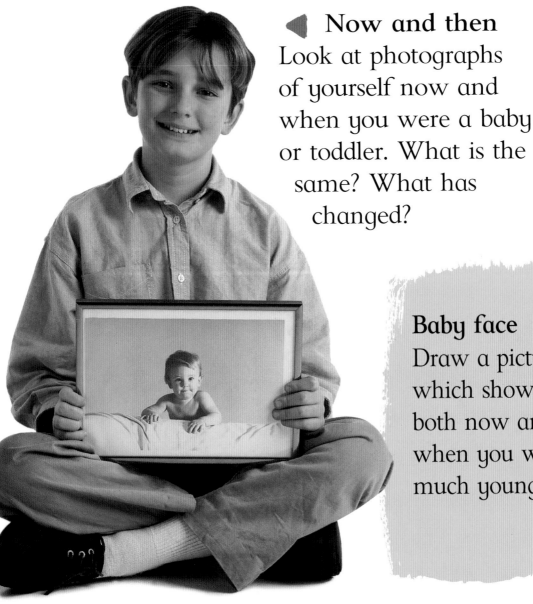

◀ Now and then
Look at photographs of yourself now and when you were a baby or toddler. What is the same? What has changed?

Baby face
Draw a picture which shows you both now and when you were much younger.

What is odd about some of the houses and one of the people in the painting?

▲ *I and the Village*, Marc Chagall, 1911

Chagall's self-portrait shows himself with memories of the place where he grew up. Can you find someone milking a cow?

Quiz

1. Would an artist use a mirror or a magnifying glass to study themselves for a self-portrait?

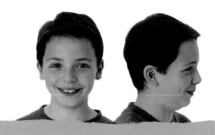

2. Which of these photos shows a profile?

3. What is a sculpted head called?

4. Find the self-portraits in the book that show artists feeling happy.

5. Look again at the self-portraits in the book and notice the details. For example, what color are this artist's eyes and mouth? What is she wearing on her head?

Glossary

bust A sculpted artwork that shows only the head and shoulders of a person.

detail The smallest lines or brushstrokes that can make a picture look more lifelike.

expression The way your face looks when you smile, cry, laugh, or feel serious.

features The eyes, eyebrows, ears, nose, mouth, and chin of a person's face.

imaginary Something that exists in the mind.

model To shape a soft material, such as clay.

pose To put your face or body in a particular position for a photograph or a painting.

profile The side view of a face.

reflection The image that you can see in a mirror.

sculpture A carved or modeled artwork that can be seen from all sides.

Websites

www.npg.org.uk
The website for the National Portrait Gallery in London allows you to search for particular self-portraits or search the entire collection for self-portraits.

www.metmuseum.org
The website of the Metropolitan Museum of Art in New York allows you to search the collection for self-portraits.

www.vangoghgallery.com
Online gallery featuring all of van Gogh's self-portraits.

Note to parents and teachers
Every effort has been made by the Publishers to ensure that these websites are suitable for children. However, because of the nature of the Internet, it is impossible to guarantee that the contents of these sites will not be altered. We strongly advise that Internet access is supervised by a responsible adult.

Index